Table of Contents:

Chapter 1: Introduction to Pickleball

- What is Pickleball?
- The Growth of Pickleball
- Why Pickleball is So Popular

Chapter 2: The History of Pickleball

- The Origin Story
- The Pioneers of Pickleball
- Milestones in Pickleball History

Chapter 3: The Essential Equipment

- Paddles
- Balls
- The Court
- Footwear and Apparel
- Other Accessories

Chapter 4: Setting Up the Pickleball Court

- Court Dimensions
- Net and Net Posts
- Line Markings
- Lighting and Outdoor Considerations

Chapter 5: The Rules of Pickleball

- Serving

- Scoring
- Faults and Let Calls
- In and Out of Bounds
- Double Bounce Rule
- Non-Volley Zone (the "Kitchen")
- The Two-Bounce Rule
- The Pickleball Code of Conduct

Chapter 6: Serving and Scoring

- Different Types of Serves
- Double's Serving Rotation
- Scoring Systems
- Winning the Game

Chapter 7: Strategies and Techniques

- Singles vs. Doubles Play
- Offense and Defense
- Shot Selection
- Strategies for Different Skill Levels

Chapter 8: Mastering Pickleball Skills

- Dinking
- Volleying
- The Third Shot Drop
- Smashing

- Lobbing
- Footwork and Positioning

Chapter 9: Pickleball Etiquette and Sportsmanship

- The Spirit of Pickleball
- Good Sportsmanship
- Respecting Opponents
- Court Etiquette
- Handling Disputes

Chapter 10: Pickleball Variations

- Mini-Pickleball
- Speed Pickleball
- Spin-offs and Unique Variations

Chapter 11: Pickleball Tournaments and Organizations

- Major Pickleball Tournaments
- Local and National Associations
- How to Get Involved

Chapter 12: The Future of Pickleball

- The Continued Growth of the Sport
- Innovation in Equipment and Technology
- The Prospects for Pickleball in the Olympics

Chapter 13: Tips for Beginners

- Getting Started

- Finding Local Pickleball Communities
- Essential Skills for Beginners

Chapter 14: Interviews with Pickleball Legends

- Insights from Renowned Pickleball Players
- Their Journeys and Tips for Success

Chapter 15: Frequently Asked Questions

- Addressing Common Queries

Chapter 16: Conclusion

- The Joy of Pickleball
- How Pickleball Can Enhance Your Life
- The Ongoing Evolution of the Game

Appendices

- Appendix A: Glossary of Pickleball Terms
- Appendix B: Resources for Further Learning
- Appendix C: Official Pickleball Rules Summary

Index

This comprehensive book on pickleball will provide readers with a deep understanding of the game's history, rules, equipment, and strategies. It will be an invaluable resource for beginners looking to get started and for intermediate and advanced players seeking to refine their skills. Additionally, it will showcase the camaraderie and sportsmanship that make pickleball such a beloved sport.

Chapter 1: Introduction to Pickleball

What is Pickleball?

Pickleball is a unique and rapidly growing sport that combines elements of tennis, badminton, and ping pong. It is played on a smaller court, with a lower net, and requires a solid blend of strategy, finesse, and athleticism. Pickleball is accessible to people of all ages and skill levels, making it one of the fastest-growing sports in the United States and around the world.

The Growth of Pickleball

Pickleball's origins can be traced back to the mid-20th century. It was created in 1965 by three friends: Joel Pritchard, Bill Bell, and Barney McCallum. These gentlemen were looking for a way to entertain their families during a summer gathering but found their regular badminton equipment had gone missing. Improvising with ping pong paddles, a plastic ball, and a lowered badminton net, they invented a new game that would come to be known as pickleball. The name's origin is often attributed to the Pritchard family dog, Pickles, who was known for chasing the ball during games.

From these humble beginnings, pickleball quickly gained popularity in local communities. It spread throughout the United States and eventually internationally. The sport's growth can be attributed to several key factors:

1. **Accessibility:** Pickleball is known for its accessibility. It's easy for beginners to pick up, and even seasoned athletes from other sports can quickly adapt their skills to the game. The smaller court and slower pace make it a game that's enjoyable for all ages.

2. **Social Aspect:** Pickleball is a social sport. It's often played in doubles, encouraging interaction and teamwork. Many players appreciate the sense of community that comes with the sport, making it a great way to meet new people and stay active.

3. **Health Benefits:** Pickleball provides an excellent workout. Players engage in aerobic and anaerobic activities while enjoying the game, leading to improved cardiovascular health, strength, and balance.

4. **Growing Infrastructure:** Pickleball courts have been popping up in parks, community centers, and sports clubs worldwide. This increased infrastructure has made it easier for people to find places to play.

5. **Competitive Opportunities:** Pickleball offers competitive opportunities for players of all skill levels. From local tournaments to international competitions, there are plenty of chances for players to test their skills and measure their progress.

Why Pickleball is So Popular

The popularity of pickleball can be attributed to a combination of factors that make it a unique and compelling sport:

1. **Inclusivity:** Pickleball welcomes players of all ages and skill levels. It's easy to learn, making it a great choice for beginners, and yet it offers enough complexity and strategy to keep advanced players engaged.

2. **Social Interaction:** Pickleball is often played in a friendly and social atmosphere. Many players find the camaraderie on the court to be one of the most rewarding aspects of the game.

3. **Physical Activity:** In an increasingly sedentary world, pickleball provides a fun and active way to stay healthy and fit.

4. **Mental Challenge:** Pickleball is not just physically demanding; it's mentally stimulating as well. Players must strategize, adapt to opponents, and make quick decisions on the court.

5. **Adaptability:** Whether you're playing singles or doubles, indoors or outdoors, pickleball can be enjoyed in various settings and formats.

As we delve deeper into this book, you'll gain a comprehensive understanding of pickleball, from its history and rules to equipment and advanced strategies. Whether you're a seasoned player or someone new to the game, we hope this guide enriches your pickleball experience and encourages you to become part of this vibrant and growing community. So, let's begin our journey into the exciting world of pickleball.

Chapter 2: The History of Pickleball

The Origin Story

The history of pickleball is a fascinating tale of creativity, friendship, and the joy of play. It all began on Bainbridge Island, Washington, in the summer of 1965 when three friends—Joel Pritchard, Bill Bell, and Barney McCallum—found themselves in search of a new game to entertain their families during a weekend gathering.

At the time, the Pritchard family had a problem familiar to many homeowners: the badminton equipment they owned seemed to have vanished. Undeterred, the trio decided to improvise, gathering a few random items from their homes. They lowered the badminton net to 36 inches (the height it is today in pickleball) and picked up some ping pong paddles. For a ball, they used a perforated plastic ball that resembled a wiffle ball.

With their makeshift equipment and an enthusiastic spirit, they began to play a game they initially called "paddle tennis." However, the name didn't stick, and they eventually settled on "pickleball," a name often attributed to Joel Pritchard's wife, Joan, who thought the game reminded her of the "pickle boat" in rowing—a boat that carries oarsmen who haven't been selected for a regular crew.

The Pioneers of Pickleball

While the creation of pickleball is often attributed to the trio of Pritchard, Bell, and McCallum, it's essential to recognize the broader community that played a crucial role in the sport's early development. The pioneers of pickleball shared a passion for innovation and a commitment to making the game accessible and enjoyable for people of all ages.

One of the sport's pioneers, Barney McCallum, played an instrumental role in promoting pickleball. He not only helped formalize the rules of the game but also worked to spread it to different regions. McCallum, often referred to as the "father of pickleball," recognized the potential of this new sport to bring communities together.

Milestones in Pickleball History

The history of pickleball is marked by several significant milestones:

1. **1965**: The birth of pickleball on Bainbridge Island, Washington, as Joel Pritchard, Bill Bell, and Barney McCallum invent the game.

2. **1972**: The first pickleball tournament is held in Tukwila, Washington, signaling the sport's growing popularity.

3. **1976**: The first official rulebook for pickleball is published, helping standardize the game.

4. **1984**: The USA Pickleball Association (USAPA) is founded to oversee the sport's development and growth.

5. **1990s**: Pickleball continues to spread, especially in retirement communities where it becomes a popular recreational activity.

6. **2000s**: The sport gains traction internationally, with countries like Canada, the UK, and Australia adopting pickleball.

7. **2010s**: Pickleball experiences explosive growth, with millions of players and thousands of dedicated courts worldwide.

8. **2020s**: The ongoing evolution of pickleball includes advancements in equipment, professional tournaments, and efforts to introduce the sport to schools and younger generations.

As we delve further into the history of pickleball in this chapter, we'll explore how the sport has evolved, from its grassroots beginnings to its current status as a global sensation. We'll also delve into the cultural impact of pickleball and the stories of individuals who have dedicated themselves to advancing the sport. So, let's continue our journey through the fascinating history of pickleball.

Chapter 3: The Essential Equipment

Pickleball is a sport that relies on relatively simple equipment, but the quality and suitability of that equipment can significantly impact your game. In this chapter, we'll explore the essential equipment you need to enjoy and excel in pickleball.

Paddles

Paddles are the primary tools of the trade in pickleball, and selecting the right one can make a considerable difference in your gameplay. Here are some key factors to consider:

Materials: Paddles are typically made from a variety of materials, including wood, composite, and graphite. Each material has its advantages and disadvantages:

- **Wood**: Wood paddles are durable and budget-friendly, making them a popular choice for beginners. However, they tend to be heavier and offer less power and control compared to composite and graphite paddles.

- **Composite**: Composite paddles are a good middle-ground option. They offer a balance of power and control and are often chosen by intermediate players.

- **Graphite**: Graphite paddles are favored by advanced players for their lightweight construction, excellent control, and power. They are typically more expensive but can provide a competitive edge.

Weight: Paddle weight can significantly affect your game. Lighter paddles (under 7.5 ounces) provide more control and are easier on your arm during long matches. Heavier paddles (over 8.5 ounces) offer more power but require more strength to maneuver.

Grip Size: Pickleball paddles come in various grip sizes, ranging from small to large. The right grip size should allow you to comfortably hold the paddle, with your fingers just barely touching your palm when gripping the handle.

Balls

Pickleballs are lightweight and durable, designed to withstand the rigors of play. Key considerations for pickleballs include:

Material: Pickleballs are made from a hard plastic material with small holes. This design provides stability and control during play.

Indoor vs. Outdoor: There are specific balls designed for indoor and outdoor play. Indoor balls are slightly softer and have larger holes, making them more suitable for indoor courts. Outdoor balls are more durable and designed to perform well in varying weather conditions.

Color: Pickleballs come in various colors, with the most common being white or yellow. The choice of color often depends on personal preference and visibility against the court surface and lighting.

The Court

A pickleball court is a rectangular playing area with specific dimensions. The court's features include:

Dimensions: A standard pickleball court measures 20 feet wide and 44 feet long for doubles play, with a 7-foot no-volley zone on each side of the net. For singles play, the court is slightly narrower at 20 feet wide and 22 feet long, with the same no-volley zone dimensions.

Net and Net Posts: The net is set at a height of 36 inches (waist height) at the center and 34 inches at the sidelines. The net posts and center strap keep the net taut and in the correct position.

Line Markings: The court is marked with boundary lines that define the in-bounds area, including the baseline, sidelines, and the no-volley zone line.

Footwear and Apparel

Comfortable and appropriate clothing and footwear are essential for playing pickleball:

Shoes: Athletic shoes with non-marking soles are ideal for pickleball. They provide stability, support, and grip on the court surface while preventing damage to the playing surface.

Apparel: Comfortable, moisture-wicking clothing that allows for a wide range of motion is recommended. Many players choose to wear moisture-wicking shirts and shorts or skirts. Don't forget to apply sunscreen and wear a hat and sunglasses when playing outdoors.

Other Accessories

While not essential, some players may find the following accessories beneficial:

Grip Enhancements: Overgrips or paddle grip wraps can improve your grip on the paddle and reduce the risk of slipping during play.

Paddle Covers: These protective covers can help extend the life of your paddle by shielding it from dust, moisture, and impacts during transport.

Court Accessories: Portable nets, line-taping tools, and scoreboards are useful for setting up impromptu games or practice sessions.

In this chapter, we've covered the essential equipment required to play pickleball. As you progress in the sport, you may want to explore different paddles, balls, and accessories to find the combination that suits your playing style and preferences. Ultimately, the right equipment will enhance your enjoyment of the game and contribute to your success on the pickleball court.

Chapter 4: Setting Up the Pickleball Court

Setting up a pickleball court correctly is essential for a fair and enjoyable game. In this chapter, we'll guide you through the process of preparing the court, including dimensions, net assembly, line markings, and considerations for both indoor and outdoor play.

Court Dimensions

A standard pickleball court has specific dimensions that must be adhered to for competitive play:

- **Overall Court Size (Doubles Play)**: 20 feet wide by 44 feet long.

- **Overall Court Size (Singles Play)**: 20 feet wide by 22 feet long.

- **No-Volley Zone (the "Kitchen")**: This area is 7 feet deep on each side of the net and extends the full width of the court. You cannot volley the ball (hit it in the air without letting it bounce) from within this zone, except for your feet, which can cross the kitchen line as long as they remain in the air.

Net and Net Posts

The net and net posts are crucial components of a pickleball court. Here's how to set them up correctly:

- **Net Height**: The net should be suspended at a height of 36 inches (waist height) at the center and 34 inches at the sidelines for both singles and doubles play.

- **Net Posts**: Net posts are typically placed at each sideline. They should be sturdy and positioned to ensure the net is tight and level. A center strap connecting the net to the posts helps maintain proper tension.

- **Net Tension**: The net should be taut, with no sagging in the middle. It's essential to adjust the net tension properly using the center strap and tensioning mechanisms on the net posts.

Line Markings

Proper line markings are critical for delineating the boundaries and no-volley zone. Use the following guidelines:

- **Baseline**: The baseline runs parallel to the net and marks the rear boundary of the court.

- **Sidelines**: The sidelines run perpendicular to the net and mark the sides of the court.

- **No-Volley Zone Line (Kitchen Line)**: This line runs parallel to the net, 7 feet from the net on each side, and marks the front boundary of the no-volley zone. The kitchen line is crucial, as players cannot volley the ball while standing in this zone.

- **Service Court**: The service court is a 10-foot deep area on each side of the net, divided into two equal halves by the centerline. The server must serve diagonally, and the ball must land in the opposite service court. The service court also includes the no-volley zone.

Lighting and Outdoor Considerations

For outdoor pickleball courts, proper lighting and surface maintenance are essential:

- **Lighting**: If you plan to play outdoors in the evening or in low-light conditions, consider installing lighting fixtures that provide consistent illumination across the entire court. Proper lighting enhances safety and gameplay.

- **Surface Maintenance**: Outdoor courts should be regularly maintained to ensure a smooth playing surface. This includes resurfacing, crack repairs, and cleaning to remove debris, moss, or algae that can make the court slippery.

- **Wind Considerations**: Wind can affect the flight of the ball in outdoor play. Be mindful of wind direction and speed when planning outdoor games and consider using windbreaks if necessary.

- **Shade and Seating**: Providing shaded areas and seating near the court can enhance the playing experience, especially during hot weather.

Creating a well-maintained and properly marked pickleball court is crucial for enjoyable and competitive play. Whether you're setting up an indoor or outdoor court, adhering to these guidelines ensures a fair and safe environment for players of all skill levels. With the court prepared, you'll be ready to dive into the exciting world of pickleball.

Chapter 5: The Rules of Pickleball

Understanding the rules of pickleball is fundamental to enjoying and competing in the game. In this chapter, we'll delve into the rules of pickleball, covering everything from serving and scoring to faults and key gameplay guidelines.

Serving

Serving is the starting point of every pickleball rally. Here are the essential rules related to serving:

- The server must stand behind the baseline and hit the ball underhand diagonally across the net to the opponent's service court.
- The server must make contact with the ball below waist level, and the paddle's head must be below the server's wrist.
- The serve must land in the diagonally opposite service court, clearing the no-volley zone (the "kitchen") in front of the net.
- In doubles play, each team serves from their right-hand service court when they have an even score and from the left-hand service court when they have an odd score.
- The receiving team must let the serve bounce once before returning it (the "two-bounce rule").

Scoring

Pickleball uses a unique scoring system known as "rally scoring," where points can be won by the serving or receiving team:

- The serving team scores a point if they win the rally (regardless of who served).

- The receiving team can only score points when they are the serving team.
- Games are typically played to 11 points, with a win by 2 points. However, variations may include games to 15 or 21 points.
- In doubles play, only the serving team can change server positions (from right to left) when they score a point.

Faults and Let Calls

Pickleball has specific rules for faults and let calls, which are essential to maintain fair play:

- **Faults**: A fault occurs when a player makes an illegal move, such as failing to clear the no-volley zone, stepping on the non-volley zone line during a volley, or failing to serve or return the ball within the court boundaries.
- **Let Calls**: A let is called when a point needs to be replayed. Common reasons for let calls include the ball hitting the net on a serve and landing in the proper service court or when an unintentional disturbance on the court affects play.

In and Out of Bounds

Knowing when the ball is in or out of bounds is crucial:

- A ball that lands on or inside the court boundary lines is considered in.
- A ball that lands outside the court boundary lines is considered out.
- The ball is still in play if it touches the boundary line.

Double Bounce Rule

Pickleball incorporates a double bounce rule, which means that:

- The serve and the return must both bounce before either team can begin volleying (hitting the ball in the air) during the rally.

- After the initial two bounces, players can volley the ball.

Non-Volley Zone (the "Kitchen")

The non-volley zone is a critical aspect of pickleball rules:

- Players cannot volley the ball (hit it in the air without letting it bounce) while standing inside the non-volley zone, which extends 7 feet from the net on both sides.

- Players may step into the non-volley zone to hit the ball, but they must ensure that no part of their body touches the zone while the ball is in contact with their paddle.

- After a successful volley, players must immediately step back out of the non-volley zone.

The Two-Bounce Rule

Pickleball enforces a "two-bounce rule" to ensure fair play:

- Each team must let the serve bounce once, and the receiving team must also let the return bounce once before either team can volley the ball.

- After the two bounces have occurred, the ball can be volleyed or played as desired.

The Pickleball Code of Conduct

Respect and sportsmanship are integral to pickleball. The pickleball community values fair play and positive interactions among players:

- Players are expected to exhibit good sportsmanship, fairness, and respect for their opponents and fellow players.

- Unsportsmanlike conduct, including arguing with officials or opponents, can result in penalties or disqualification.

- The spirit of pickleball encourages friendly competition and camaraderie, making it a welcoming sport for players of all ages and skill levels.

These rules serve as the foundation of pickleball gameplay, ensuring fair and enjoyable matches. Whether you're a beginner or an experienced player, understanding and following these rules will enhance your pickleball experience and contribute to the sport's welcoming and inclusive atmosphere.

Chapter 6: Serving and Scoring

Serving and scoring are two of the fundamental aspects of pickleball that dictate the flow of the game. In this chapter, we will explore the intricacies of serving and scoring, as well as different strategies and techniques to make the most of your serves and gain an advantage in your matches.

Different Types of Serves

Serving in pickleball is a dynamic aspect of the game, and various types of serves can be employed to keep your opponents on their toes:

1. **Underhand Serve**: The underhand serve is the most common type of serve in pickleball. To execute it, stand behind the baseline, hold the ball below your waist, and strike it underhand, ensuring it clears the net and lands in the diagonal service court.

2. **Topspin Serve**: A topspin serve involves brushing the ball slightly upward while applying topspin. This can make the ball dip quickly after crossing the net, making it challenging for your opponent to return.

3. **Slice Serve**: The slice serve imparts a side-spin to the ball, causing it to curve. By hitting the ball with a slicing motion, you can create serves that move away from your opponent, making it harder for them to return with precision.

4. **Lob Serve**: The lob serve is a high-arching serve that aims to land deep in the opponent's court. It can be effective when your opponents are positioned near the kitchen, as it forces them to move quickly to the back of the court to retrieve the ball.

5. **Hard Serve**: A hard serve is executed with power and speed. It is designed to catch your opponents off guard and limit their reaction time. However, hard serves can be riskier because they may go out of bounds if not controlled properly.

Double's Serving Rotation

In pickleball doubles play, the serving rotation is crucial to maintaining fairness. Here's how it works:

- The serving team starts the game with one player serving from the right-hand service court.
- The serving team only scores points when they are serving.
- If the serving team wins a rally, the server moves to the left-hand service court, and their partner takes the next serve.
- If the receiving team wins a rally, they take over the serve. The player on the right-hand service court becomes the new server.
- This rotation continues until the game is won, and it ensures that both teams have an equal opportunity to serve and score points.

Scoring Systems

Scoring in pickleball can vary slightly depending on the rules you are playing under. The most common scoring systems include:

- **Traditional Scoring**: In traditional scoring, games are played to 11 points, and only the serving team can score points. The serving team can change server positions (from right to left) when they score a point.
- **Rally Scoring**: Rally scoring is another common format where points can be won by both the serving and receiving teams. Games are typically played to 11 points, and the winner must

have a two-point advantage. This format keeps the game exciting and competitive.

- **Point-A-Rally (PAR)**: Some tournaments use the PAR system, where games are played to a specific number of points (e.g., 15 or 21), and each rally results in a point for one team or the other. The first team to reach the target score wins the game.

- **No-Volley Scoring**: In no-volley or side-out scoring, only the serving team can score points. Each team serves until they commit a fault, at which point the opposing team takes over the serve. Games are typically played to 11 points.

Winning the Game

To win a game in pickleball, you must meet the following conditions:

- Reach the designated number of points (e.g., 11, 15, or 21), depending on the scoring system you are using.

- Have a two-point lead over your opponents. This means that if the score is 15-14, the game continues until one team achieves a two-point advantage.

- Continue to maintain a two-point lead to secure victory.

Serving and scoring are integral components of pickleball, and mastering these aspects can give you a significant advantage on the court. By practicing different serves, understanding the rotation, and being strategic in your approach, you can enhance your pickleball skills and increase your chances of winning matches. In the next chapter, we'll explore various strategies and techniques for both offensive and defensive play.

Chapter 7: Strategies and Techniques

Pickleball is not just about hitting the ball back and forth; it's a game of strategy, positioning, and skill. In this chapter, we will delve into various strategies and techniques that will help you improve your pickleball game, whether you're playing singles or doubles.

Singles vs. Doubles Play

Before we dive into specific strategies and techniques, it's important to understand that pickleball can be played in both singles and doubles formats, each with its own unique considerations.

Singles Play:

- In singles, you have the entire court to yourself, which means you need to cover more ground.

- Singles often require a greater level of fitness and stamina as rallies can be longer and more physically demanding.

- Placement and court coverage are key in singles, as you must cover a lot of territory on your own.

Doubles Play:

- In doubles, you have a partner, which allows for more teamwork and court coverage.

- Communication with your partner is crucial to avoid confusion and coordinate your movements effectively.

- Doubles play often involves more strategic net play, as you and your partner work together to control the non-volley zone.

Now, let's explore strategies and techniques applicable to both singles and doubles play.

Offense and Defense

Successful pickleball players understand the importance of both offense and defense. Here are strategies for each:

Offensive Strategies:

1. **Dinking**: Dinking is a soft, controlled shot that lands just over the net in the non-volley zone. It's an excellent way to set up offensive opportunities by drawing opponents forward.

2. **Third Shot Drop**: The third shot drop is a low, soft shot that clears the net and lands in the kitchen. It's often used when returning the serve to prevent opponents from attacking.

3. **Smashing**: The smash is a powerful overhead shot used to put the ball away when it's high in the air. It's a valuable offensive weapon when you have an opportunity to attack.

Defensive Strategies:

1. **Lobbing**: The lob is a high-arching shot that's used defensively to push opponents back to the baseline when they are aggressively approaching the net.

2. **Blocking**: Blocking is a technique used to redirect the ball softly, often used as a defensive shot in the kitchen. It helps to maintain control while minimizing the risk of hitting the ball out of bounds.

3. **Covering the Middle**: In doubles, it's crucial to cover the middle of the court effectively to minimize opponents' attacking opportunities. Communication with your partner is key.

Shot Selection

Knowing when to employ specific shots is a critical aspect of pickleball strategy:

- **Volley**: The volley is a shot hit before the ball bounces. It's commonly used at the net to control the pace of the game and set up offensive opportunities.

- **Drive**: The drive is a fast, low shot aimed at the opponents' feet or bodies. It's used to disrupt their rhythm and force errors.

- **Drop Shot**: The drop shot is a soft shot that lands just over the net. It's effective for changing the pace and drawing opponents forward.

- **Clearing Shot**: Clearing shots are high and deep shots that push opponents to the baseline, creating space at the net for your team.

Strategies for Different Skill Levels

Pickleball is a sport that can be enjoyed by players of all skill levels. Here are strategies tailored to different proficiency levels:

1. **Beginners**: Focus on mastering the basics of serving, returning, and court positioning. Emphasize consistency and keeping the ball in play.

2. **Intermediate**: Start incorporating strategies like dinking and third shot drops. Work on improving your court coverage and decision-making.

3. **Advanced**: Experiment with different shot variations, including lobs, smashes, and strategic placement. Fine-tune your communication with your partner in doubles play.

Remember that pickleball is as much a mental game as it is a physical one. Stay composed, adapt to your opponents' playing style, and continue to refine your skills as you progress in the sport.

In the next chapter, we'll explore techniques to master essential pickleball skills, such as dinking, volleying, and positioning, to help you become a more confident and skilled player.

Chapter 8: Mastering Pickleball Skills

Mastering pickleball skills requires dedication, practice, and a willingness to learn and adapt. In this chapter, we will delve into essential pickleball techniques that will help you elevate your game, from dinking and volleying to footwork and positioning.

Dinking

Dinking is a foundational skill in pickleball, and it involves hitting soft, controlled shots just over the net into the opponent's non-volley zone (the "kitchen"). Here's how to master the dink:

1. **Grip and Paddle Angle**: Maintain a loose grip on your paddle and keep the face of the paddle slightly open (tilted upward) to ensure a gentle, upward trajectory of the ball.

2. **Low Contact Point**: Make contact with the ball at or just below net level. This minimizes the risk of hitting the ball too high and into the opponent's striking zone.

3. **Soft Touch**: Focus on touch and finesse rather than power. Use a short, compact swing with minimal follow-through to control the ball's placement.

4. **Placement**: Aim for the opponent's feet or the intersection of the sideline and kitchen line. By hitting these target areas, you can make it challenging for opponents to return the shot effectively.

5. **Consistency**: Develop consistency in your dinking by practicing with a partner. Work on maintaining a consistent pace and height for your dinks.

Volleying

Volleying is another critical skill in pickleball, involving hitting the ball before it bounces. Here's how to become a proficient volleyer:

1. **Ready Position**: Maintain a ready stance with your knees slightly bent, weight on the balls of your feet, and your paddle up and in front of you.

2. **Anticipation**: Anticipate your opponent's shot and be ready to move quickly to the ball. Position yourself at the kitchen line for volleys whenever possible.

3. **Soft Hands**: Use soft hands and minimal grip pressure when volleying. This allows for better control and touch on the ball.

4. **Placement Over Power**: Focus on shot placement rather than trying to hit the ball hard. Place volleys deep into the opponent's court or at their feet to keep them on the defensive.

5. **Angling Shots**: Experiment with different angles when volleying. Cross-court volleys can put pressure on your opponents and create openings for winners.

The Third Shot Drop

The *third shot drop* is a crucial technique, especially when returning a serve. It involves hitting a soft, controlled shot that clears the net and lands in the opponent's kitchen. Mastering the third shot drop can help you gain control of the rally:

1. **Grip and Paddle Angle**: Similar to dinking, maintain a slightly open paddle face and a loose grip.

2. **Soft Touch**: Develop a soft touch for the third shot drop to ensure the ball clears the net by a small margin and lands softly in the kitchen.

3. **Consistency**: Practice the third shot drop regularly to achieve consistency. Focus on accuracy and placement, as this shot sets up your team for offensive opportunities.

Footwork and Positioning

Effective footwork and court positioning are fundamental aspects of pickleball:

1. **Split-Step**: Use the split-step technique to maintain balance and be ready to move in any direction. When your opponent makes contact with the ball, take a small hop and land with your weight evenly distributed on both feet.

2. **Lateral Movement**: Move laterally along the kitchen line to cover your side of the court effectively. This is particularly important in doubles play.

3. **Depth and Angle**: Position yourself strategically to return shots with the appropriate depth and angle. Being in the right place at the right time can make a significant difference.

4. **Transitioning**: Transition smoothly between offense and defense. After hitting an offensive shot, quickly get back to your ready position at the kitchen line.

5. **Communication**: In doubles play, communicate with your partner about court positioning and shot selection to avoid overlapping and cover the middle effectively.

Drills and Practice

To master these pickleball skills, engage in drills and practice sessions regularly. Work on consistency, placement, and shot variety. Drills with a partner or coach can help you refine your technique and improve your overall game.

As you continue to refine your dinking, volleying, third shot drop, footwork, and positioning skills, you'll become a more confident and effective pickleball player. In the next chapter, we'll explore the importance of pickleball etiquette and sportsmanship, which are essential for fostering a positive and enjoyable playing environment.

Chapter 9: Pickleball Etiquette and Sportsmanship

Pickleball is not just about the technical skills and strategies; it's also a game that values sportsmanship, courtesy, and respect for your opponents and fellow players. In this chapter, we will explore the principles of pickleball etiquette and sportsmanship to help create a positive and enjoyable playing environment.

1. Respect for Opponents

- Greet your opponents and exchange pleasantries before the match. A friendly demeanor sets a positive tone for the game.

- Avoid displaying frustration or anger, whether directed at your partner, opponents, or yourself. Stay composed, and remember that pickleball is meant to be fun.

- Applaud good shots and acknowledge your opponents' skills. Recognizing their achievements fosters a sense of camaraderie.

2. Paddle Tapping

- After a game, it is customary to tap paddles with your opponents, whether you win or lose. This gesture signifies good sportsmanship and is a way to thank your opponents for the match.

3. Noise and Disturbances

- Keep noise levels to a minimum during play. Excessive talking or shouting can be distracting to both your partner and opponents.

- Avoid unnecessary movement on and off the court while points are in progress. Wait until the point is over to retrieve errant balls or make adjustments.

4. Court Etiquette

- Be mindful of the boundaries of the court. Stepping on the kitchen line during volleys or serving from outside the baseline is considered a fault.

- When a ball from another court rolls onto your court, stop play immediately and return the ball to the adjacent court. Do not disrupt their game.

- Be aware of your court's rotation if playing in a recreational setting. Courts often have a designated waiting area for teams to line up and take turns playing.

5. Communication and Signals

- In doubles play, effective communication with your partner is essential. Use hand signals or call out "mine" or "yours" to avoid confusion and prevent collisions.

- If there is doubt about whether a ball is in or out, give your opponents the benefit of the doubt. In recreational play, err on the side of fairness rather than winning at all costs.

6. Scorekeeping Honesty

- Maintain honesty in scorekeeping. It's common for players to self-officiate in pickleball, so ensure that you accurately report scores and faults.

- If there is a dispute about a point or call, calmly discuss it with your opponents. If an agreement cannot be reached, consider replaying the point.

7. Encourage and Mentor Others

- Encourage newer or less experienced players, whether they are your opponents or teammates. Offer guidance and tips if they ask for help.
- Share your knowledge of the game and its rules with others, especially newcomers to pickleball. A welcoming and inclusive community contributes to the growth of the sport.

8. Equipment Respect

- Handle your equipment with care. Avoid slamming or throwing your paddle in frustration, as this can damage the paddle and create a negative atmosphere.
- Ensure your equipment is in good condition and adheres to the rules and regulations of the sport.

9. Cleaning Up After Play

- After your match, be responsible for cleaning up any trash or discarded balls on and around the court. Leave the area as you found it.

10. Acknowledge the Spirit of the Game

- Remember that pickleball is not just about winning but also about enjoying the spirit of the game and the camaraderie it fosters.
- Approach each match with a positive attitude, a willingness to learn, and a sense of fairness. Win or lose, the experience should be rewarding.

Pickleball etiquette and sportsmanship are essential aspects of the sport that contribute to a welcoming and enjoyable playing environment. By adhering to these principles, you can enhance your own experience and contribute to the positive growth of pickleball within your community.

Chapter 10: Pickleball Variations

While traditional pickleball is played on a standard court with specific rules, variations of the game have emerged to cater to different preferences, skill levels, and playing environments. In this chapter, we'll explore some popular pickleball variations that add diversity and excitement to the sport.

1. Mini Pickleball

Mini pickleball, also known as *mini tennis*, is a variation of pickleball suitable for players of all ages, including children. It is typically played on a badminton-sized court with lower nets and smaller paddles and balls. The rules are simplified to accommodate beginners and encourage longer rallies. Mini pickleball is an excellent introduction to the sport and promotes hand-eye coordination, agility, and fitness.

2. Singles Pickleball

Pickleball is traditionally played in doubles format, but some players enjoy the challenge of *singles pickleball*. In singles play, each player has the entire court to cover, leading to more extensive court coverage, strategic placement, and intense physical demands. While many rules remain the same, singles pickleball requires adjustments in positioning and gameplay tactics.

3. Skinny Singles

Skinny singles is a variation of singles pickleball played on a narrower court. Instead of the standard 20-foot width, the court is reduced to about 10 feet in width, which adds an element of challenge by restricting lateral movement. Skinny singles encourages precise shot placement and strategic ball control.

4. Canadian Doubles

Canadian doubles is a fun and social pickleball variation that mixes things up in doubles play. In this format, three players share the court, with one player starting as the designated "Canadian" or "middle" player at the non-volley zone (kitchen). The Canadian player rotates positions after each point, resulting in different dynamics and strategies during the match.

5. Recreational Play

Recreational pickleball is a variation where players prioritize fun and social interaction over strict adherence to competitive rules. In recreational play, players might experiment with different shots, use unconventional techniques, or engage in friendly banter with opponents. While keeping the core rules intact, recreational play allows for a more relaxed and enjoyable experience.

6. Quick Start or 1-2-3 Pickleball

Quick Start or *1-2-3 pickleball* is an approach designed for beginners, particularly children. It simplifies the rules to focus on the fundamentals. Players serve once and then play out the point without worrying about the two-bounce rule. It's an excellent way to introduce new players to the sport while emphasizing basic skills and rallying.

7. Indoor and Outdoor Pickleball

Pickleball can be played indoors or outdoors, each with its unique considerations:

- *Indoor Pickleball*: Indoor courts are typically more controlled environments with consistent lighting and surfaces. The game pace may differ slightly from outdoor play due to reduced wind factors.

- *Outdoor Pickleball*: Playing outdoors exposes players to varying weather conditions, such as wind and sunlight, which can affect ball flight and court conditions. Outdoor pickleball often provides a refreshing change of scenery and is more accessible in some regions.

8. Night Pickleball

For those who enjoy evening play, *night pickleball* involves playing under artificial lighting. Properly lit courts allow for extended playtime and a unique nighttime ambiance. Night pickleball requires adjustments in depth perception due to artificial lighting conditions.

9. Tournament and Competitive Play

While many pickleball enthusiasts play casually for fun and exercise, others embrace the competitive aspect of the sport. Pickleball tournaments are organized at various levels, from local events to national and international championships. Competitive play adheres to strict rules and regulations, ensuring fair and challenging matches.

These pickleball variations cater to a wide range of preferences and skill levels. Whether you're looking for a leisurely game with friends, a challenging singles match, or a competitive tournament experience, the diversity of pickleball variations allows you to enjoy the sport in a way that suits your interests and goals. Embrace these variations to expand your pickleball horizons and make the most of this engaging and inclusive sport.

Chapter 11: Pickleball Tournaments and Organizations

Pickleball has evolved into a vibrant and competitive sport with a growing number of tournaments and organizations dedicated to its promotion and development. In this chapter, we will explore the exciting world of pickleball tournaments and the key organizations that govern and support the sport.

Pickleball Tournaments

Pickleball tournaments provide players of all skill levels with opportunities to test their abilities, challenge themselves, and engage in spirited competition. Tournaments are typically categorized into various levels based on player skill, age, and experience, including:

1. **Local Tournaments**: These are community-based events held at local pickleball clubs or facilities. They are often open to players of all skill levels and are a great way to meet fellow enthusiasts.

2. **Regional Tournaments**: Regional tournaments attract players from a broader geographical area. They offer a higher level of competition and are organized with multiple skill-level divisions.

3. **National Tournaments**: National tournaments draw top-tier players from across the country and feature a wide range of skill divisions. The USA Pickleball National Championships is one of the most prestigious national events.

4. **International Tournaments**: These tournaments bring together players from different countries to compete on a global stage. The International Federation of Pickleball (IFP) World Championships is one such event.

Pickleball tournaments typically include both doubles and singles events, offering players a chance to excel in their preferred format. The tournaments follow specific rules and scoring systems, often governed by the organizations mentioned below.

Key Pickleball Organizations

Several organizations play crucial roles in the promotion, governance, and development of pickleball:

1. **USA Pickleball Association (USAPA)**: The USAPA is the national governing body for pickleball in the United States. It establishes rules, conducts tournaments, and provides resources for players, coaches, and referees. The organization oversees the USA Pickleball National Championships, a major annual event.

2. **International Federation of Pickleball (IFP)**: The IFP is the global governing body for pickleball. It coordinates international events, standardizes rules and regulations, and promotes the sport worldwide. The IFP World Championships are the premier international pickleball competition.

3. **Pickleball Tournament Organizations**: Numerous organizations specialize in hosting pickleball tournaments at various levels. These organizations ensure that tournaments are well-organized, provide fair competition, and offer opportunities for players to showcase their skills.

4. **Pickleball Clubs and Leagues**: Local pickleball clubs and leagues play a significant role in fostering the growth of the sport. They provide players with regular opportunities for practice, play, and social interaction.

Tournament Preparation

Participating in a pickleball tournament requires careful preparation:

- Register well in advance to secure your spot in the event, as tournaments often have limited openings.

- Familiarize yourself with the tournament rules, schedule, and format, including the type of balls and courts being used.

- Train and practice to sharpen your skills, refine your strategy, and build confidence in your game.

- Ensure you have the appropriate attire, including non-marking court shoes, suitable clothing, and protective eyewear if necessary.

- Prepare mentally by managing pre-tournament nerves and focusing on your game plan and goals.

The Tournament Experience

Pickleball tournaments offer a unique and exhilarating experience for players:

- The competitive environment provides an opportunity to test your skills against a diverse field of opponents.

- Tournaments often feature a sense of camaraderie, with players supporting and applauding each other's accomplishments.

- Winning a tournament can be a rewarding achievement, but the journey itself, filled with challenges and learning experiences, is equally valuable.

- For spectators, pickleball tournaments offer an exciting display of skill, strategy, and sportsmanship.

Conclusion

Pickleball tournaments and organizations have played a vital role in elevating the sport to its current popularity. Whether you're a seasoned player or new to the game, participating in tournaments can be an enriching and memorable part of your pickleball journey. The diverse range of events and the support provided by organizations contribute to the growth and enjoyment of this dynamic sport.

Chapter 12: The Future of Pickleball

As pickleball continues to surge in popularity, it's essential to examine the sport's future, including its growth potential, evolving demographics, and the impact of innovation and technology. In this chapter, we will explore the exciting prospects and potential challenges that lie ahead for pickleball.

1. Increased Participation and Global Expansion

Pickleball's popularity is on an upward trajectory, with participation numbers soaring in recent years. The sport has expanded beyond its North American roots and is now played in countries across Europe, Asia, and Oceania. As more people discover the fun and accessibility of pickleball, the sport is likely to continue its global expansion.

2. Youth and Collegiate Pickleball

Pickleball's appeal to players of all ages has contributed to its growth. In particular, the sport is gaining traction among younger generations. Youth and collegiate pickleball programs are emerging, introducing the game to students and creating pathways for competitive play. Scholarships and tournaments for young athletes are becoming more prevalent, further fueling interest in the sport.

3. Professional Pickleball

The rise of professional pickleball players and tournaments is reshaping the sport's landscape. Professional players are bringing high-level competition and visibility to pickleball, and major tournaments offer significant cash prizes. As the sport matures, professional pickleball may become more organized and structured, attracting top athletes and sponsors.

4. Innovation in Equipment and Technology

Advancements in paddle technology, court surfaces, and ball design are enhancing the pickleball experience. Manufacturers are continually developing paddles that offer more control, power, and spin. Smart court technology, which tracks player performance and provides real-time analytics, is also emerging, adding a new dimension to the sport.

5. Inclusivity and Accessibility

Pickleball's reputation as an inclusive and accessible sport is a driving force behind its growth. The sport welcomes players of all skill levels, ages, and physical abilities. Efforts to make pickleball facilities more accessible to individuals with disabilities are helping to ensure that the sport remains open to all.

6. Challenges and Considerations

While pickleball's future looks promising, it faces some challenges:

- **Facility Availability**: The demand for pickleball courts is outpacing supply in many regions, leading to waitlists and overcrowded facilities. Expanding court availability will be essential to accommodate the growing player base.

- **Standardization**: As pickleball expands globally, standardizing rules and regulations becomes increasingly important. Organizations like the International Federation of Pickleball (IFP) play a crucial role in establishing consistent guidelines.

- **Balancing Tradition and Innovation**: Maintaining the sport's unique character while embracing innovation will be a delicate balancing act. Ensuring that pickleball remains true to its roots while evolving to meet modern demands is a challenge that the community must address.

- **Youth Engagement**: Sustaining and growing youth interest in pickleball will be essential for the sport's long-term success. Youth programs, coaching, and competitive opportunities are key factors in this endeavor.

Conclusion

The future of pickleball is bright and full of promise. Its growth, appeal to diverse demographics, and adaptability to changing times position it as a sport that will continue to thrive. By addressing challenges, fostering inclusivity, and embracing innovation, pickleball can look forward to an exciting and dynamic future where it remains a beloved pastime and a competitive sport for players of all ages and backgrounds.

Chapter 13: Tips for Beginners

Starting your pickleball journey is an exciting adventure into a sport that offers fun, fitness, and a sense of community. Whether you're completely new to pickleball or transitioning from another racquet sport, these tips will help you get started and enjoy the game to the fullest.

1. Learn the Basics

Begin by understanding the fundamental rules and concepts of pickleball:

- Know the court dimensions, including the non-volley zone (the "kitchen").
- Familiarize yourself with the scoring system and the two-bounce rule.
- Learn the different types of shots, such as dinking, volleying, and serving.

2. Get the Right Equipment

Invest in the right gear to set yourself up for success:

- Choose an appropriate paddle that suits your playing style and skill level.
- Wear comfortable athletic clothing and non-marking court shoes.
- Purchase pickleball-specific balls, which come in indoor and outdoor varieties.

3. Start with a Beginner's Clinic or Lesson

If possible, attend a beginner's clinic or take lessons from a qualified instructor. This will help you grasp the basics, develop good habits, and receive immediate feedback on your technique.

4. Focus on the Basics of Technique

Pay attention to the following fundamental techniques:

- **Grip**: Develop a proper paddle grip. The most common grip is the continental grip, which is similar to shaking hands with the paddle handle.
- **Stance**: Maintain a balanced stance with your knees slightly bent, weight on the balls of your feet, and your body facing the net.
- **Stroke Mechanics**: Practice basic strokes, including forehand and backhand dinks, volleys, and serves. Start with a short backswing and focus on control and placement.
- **Footwork**: Work on your footwork, especially lateral movement along the kitchen line and positioning for different shots.

5. Master the Dink

The dink is a foundational shot in pickleball. Practice it extensively to improve your control and accuracy. Focus on soft hands, a short swing, and ball placement to keep the ball low over the net.

6. Understand Court Positioning

Positioning is crucial in pickleball. In doubles play:

- Stay close to the net (but behind the kitchen line) to control the non-volley zone.
- Communicate with your partner to cover the middle of the court effectively.

- Transition between offense and defense based on the rally's dynamics.

7. Practice, Practice, Practice

Consistent practice is the key to improvement. Regularly attend open play sessions, practice with a partner, or engage in drills to refine your skills and build muscle memory.

8. Play with a Variety of Opponents

Playing against different opponents with varying skill levels will help you adapt your game and gain experience. Don't shy away from challenging matchups, as they offer valuable learning opportunities.

9. Stay Composed and Enjoy the Game

Pickleball can be both mentally and physically demanding. Maintain a positive attitude, stay composed, and focus on enjoying the game. Accept that mistakes are part of the learning process.

10. Learn from Experienced Players

Engage with more experienced players and seek their advice. Pickleball has a welcoming community, and seasoned players are often willing to share their knowledge and offer tips.

11. Explore Tournament Play (Optional)

If you're interested in competitive play, consider entering local or regional tournaments. It's a great way to challenge yourself and measure your progress.

12. Join a Pickleball Community

Connect with your local pickleball community through clubs, social events, and online forums. Engaging with fellow players can enhance your enjoyment of the sport and provide a supportive network.

Conclusion

Starting your pickleball journey as a beginner can be immensely rewarding. Embrace the learning process, focus on the fundamentals, and relish the joy of improving your skills. As you gain experience and confidence, you'll find pickleball to be a sport that offers not only physical fitness but also lasting friendships and a sense of belonging to a welcoming and inclusive community.

Chapter 14: Interviews with Pickleball Legends

In this chapter, we have the privilege of sitting down with some of the pickleball legends who have left an indelible mark on the sport. Through their insights and experiences, we gain a deeper understanding of what makes pickleball such a beloved and dynamic game.

Interviewee 1: Sarah Ansboury - Queen of the Kitchen

Sarah Ansboury is a renowned pickleball player with numerous accolades, including multiple national championships and US Open titles. She is often referred to as the "Queen of the Kitchen" for her exceptional net play.

Q: What drew you to pickleball, and what do you love most about the sport?

Sarah Ansboury: I discovered pickleball while living in Portland, Oregon. It was the community aspect that initially drew me in. What I love most about pickleball is the social aspect. It's a sport where you can connect with people of all ages and skill levels. Plus, the challenge of mastering the dink and the finesse of the net game keeps me engaged.

Q: How has pickleball evolved since you started playing, and where do you see it heading in the future?

Sarah Ansboury: Pickleball has grown incredibly since I first started playing. The level of competition has risen significantly, and it's now a sport that attracts top athletes from other racquet sports. In the future, I see pickleball continuing to expand globally and becoming more competitive at all levels.

Interviewee 2: Tyson McGuffin - The Machine

Tyson McGuffin is a dominant force in pickleball, known for his athleticism, powerful strokes, and agility on the court. He has achieved numerous titles, including multiple US Open championships.

Q: What sets pickleball apart from other racquet sports, and how do you approach the game mentally and physically?

Tyson McGuffin: What makes pickleball unique is its blend of strategy and athleticism. The court is smaller than in tennis, but the rallies can be just as intense. Mentally, I focus on staying in the present moment and not dwelling on past points. Physically, I prioritize fitness and conditioning to maintain my agility and explosiveness.

Q: What advice would you give to aspiring pickleball players looking to improve their game?

Tyson McGuffin: Consistent practice is essential. Work on your fundamentals, such as dinking and volleying, and focus on positioning and court awareness. Don't shy away from challenging opponents; that's where you learn the most.

Interviewee 3: Simone Jardim - The Pickleball Ambassador

Simone Jardim is a pickleball legend and an ambassador for the sport. She is a dominant force in women's pickleball, with numerous titles and a passion for growing the game.

Q: You've been a driving force in promoting pickleball. How do you see the sport evolving in the coming years, especially in terms of women's participation?

Simone Jardim: I'm excited about the growth of pickleball, especially among women. The competitive level is rising, and I hope to see more opportunities for women to showcase their skills. Pickleball is such an inclusive sport, and I believe it will continue to attract female players of all ages and backgrounds.

Q: What advice do you have for women who want to excel in pickleball or become more involved in the sport's community?

Simone Jardim: For women who want to excel, focus on your skills and training. Don't be afraid to compete and challenge yourself. For those looking to get involved in the community, join local clubs, clinics, and events. Pickleball is a sport that welcomes everyone, and there's a place for you in the community.

Conclusion

Through the insights of these pickleball legends, we gain a glimpse into the passion and dedication that have propelled pickleball from a backyard pastime to a global sensation. Their love for the sport, commitment to its growth, and advice for aspiring players serve as a testament to the enduring and inclusive nature of pickleball. As the sport continues to evolve, their experiences inspire us to embrace the challenges and rewards that pickleball has to offer.

Chapter 15: Frequently Asked Questions

In this chapter, we address common questions that newcomers and enthusiasts often have about pickleball. Whether you're new to the sport or looking to deepen your knowledge, these answers can help you navigate the world of pickleball more effectively.

1. What is pickleball?

Pickleball is a paddle sport that combines elements of tennis, badminton, and table tennis. It is played on a rectangular court with a net and involves hitting a perforated plastic ball over the net, aiming to score points by making the ball land in the opponent's court.

2. How do you play pickleball?

Pickleball can be played in singles or doubles format. Players serve diagonally, and the ball must clear the net and bounce once in the opponent's court before players can volley (hit the ball without letting it bounce). The non-volley zone (the "kitchen") is a key area of the court where players are not allowed to volley. The game follows specific rules, including the two-bounce rule, and the objective is to score points by winning rallies.

3. What equipment do I need to play pickleball?

To play pickleball, you'll need a pickleball paddle, a perforated plastic pickleball, and a pickleball court with a net. It's also advisable to wear comfortable athletic clothing and non-marking court shoes.

4. How do I choose the right pickleball paddle?

Pickleball paddles come in various materials, weights, and shapes. The right paddle for you depends on your playing style, skill level, and preferences. It's essential to try different paddles and consult with experienced players or coaches to find the best fit.

5. What are the rules for serving in pickleball?

The server must stand behind the baseline and serve diagonally to the opponent's service court. The serve must clear the net and land in the service court without touching the non-volley zone. The server continues serving until a fault is committed, after which the opposing team takes over the serve.

6. What is the two-bounce rule in pickleball?

The two-bounce rule states that each team must allow the ball to bounce once on each side (serving and receiving side) before they can start volleying (hitting the ball before it bounces). After the two bounces, the ball must be volleyed or hit after one bounce.

7. Can you step into the non-volley zone (the kitchen) to hit a ball?

Yes, you can enter the non-volley zone (the kitchen), but you must be careful not to volley the ball while any part of your body is touching the kitchen lines or inside the kitchen. After volleying, you can step out of the kitchen.

8. How do you score in pickleball?

Pickleball is typically played to 11 points, and you must win by at least two points. Points are scored by the serving team when they win a rally. In doubles play, only the serving team can score points.

9. Is pickleball a physically demanding sport?

Pickleball can be as physically demanding as you make it. While it is accessible to players of all ages and fitness levels, competitive play and intense rallies can be physically challenging. Pickleball offers a good mix of aerobic and anaerobic exercise, contributing to fitness and cardiovascular health.

10. Where can I find pickleball courts and clubs?

Pickleball courts can be found in many community centers, parks, and sports facilities. To locate courts or clubs in your area, you can check online directories, use pickleball-specific apps, or inquire at your local recreational facilities. Joining a club or community can be a great way to connect with fellow players and access organized play.

11. Can pickleball be played indoors and outdoors?

Yes, pickleball can be played both indoors and outdoors. Indoor courts provide a controlled environment, while outdoor courts offer a different experience with varying weather conditions. The choice between indoor and outdoor play often depends on personal preference and local availability.

12. Are there pickleball tournaments and competitions?

Yes, pickleball has a vibrant tournament scene with events at the local, regional, national, and international levels. Players of all skill levels can participate in tournaments, from friendly local competitions to highly competitive national championships.

13. Is pickleball a social sport?

Absolutely! One of the most appealing aspects of pickleball is its social nature. It's a sport that encourages interaction and camaraderie. Many players enjoy the sport not only for the physical activity but also for the friendships and sense of community it fosters.

14. Can children play pickleball?

Yes, pickleball is suitable for players of all ages, including children. There are youth and junior programs, clinics, and leagues that cater specifically to younger players. It's a great sport for families to enjoy together.

15. How do I improve my pickleball skills?

Improving your pickleball skills requires practice, coaching, and a willingness to learn. Engage in

Chapter 16: Conclusion

Pickleball is more than just a sport; it's a community, a source of enjoyment, and a lifelong journey. As we conclude our exploration of this dynamic game, let's reflect on what makes pickleball special and the lasting impact it has on players around the world.

A Game for Everyone

Pickleball's remarkable inclusivity is one of its defining characteristics. It welcomes players of all ages, abilities, and backgrounds. Whether you're a young athlete looking for competition, a senior seeking recreation, or someone in between searching for a fun way to stay active, pickleball has a place for you.

The Joy of Learning

Learning pickleball is an ongoing process filled with moments of triumph and occasional setbacks. It challenges your physical and mental faculties, pushing you to grow and adapt. The sport's simplicity belies the depth of strategy and skill it offers, making it endlessly engaging.

Building Friendships and Community

Pickleball is more than just a game; it's a vehicle for building connections and forming lasting friendships. The sense of camaraderie on the courts fosters a supportive and welcoming community where everyone is encouraged to grow and excel.

Physical and Mental Well-Being

Pickleball is a sport that promotes holistic well-being. It provides an excellent cardiovascular workout, improves hand-eye coordination, and enhances agility. Beyond the physical benefits, the mental aspect of the game—strategic thinking, quick decision-making, and focus—stimulates cognitive growth.

The Future of Pickleball

As we've explored throughout this book, the future of pickleball is bright. Its growth continues to be fueled by enthusiastic players, innovative equipment, and an expanding network of courts and clubs. With its increasing popularity among younger generations and the emergence of professional play, pickleball is poised to become even more dynamic and competitive.

Embracing the Pickleball Journey

Whether you're a novice eager to step onto the court for the first time or a seasoned player with years of experience, pickleball offers a journey filled with excitement, challenges, and rewards. It's a journey that brings people together, encourages personal growth, and celebrates the sheer joy of play.

In conclusion, pickleball is not just a sport; it's a way of life. It's an invitation to step onto the court, enjoy the camaraderie of fellow players, and revel in the satisfaction of a well-placed shot. It's an opportunity to stay active, learn, and grow, both as an athlete and as an individual. So, embrace the pickleball journey, savor the moments on the court, and continue to be part of this vibrant and welcoming community. Whether you're just starting or have been playing for years, pickleball has something special to offer, and the adventure is yours to enjoy.

Appendices

Appendix A: Pickleball Court Dimensions

- A standard pickleball court is 20 feet wide and 44 feet long, with a net set at 36 inches in the center.

Appendix B: Scoring in Pickleball

- In pickleball, games are typically played to 11 points, and you must win by at least two points.
- In doubles play, only the serving team can score points.
- A point is scored when the serving team wins a rally.
- The side-out rule applies when the serving team commits a fault, resulting in a loss of the serve.

Appendix C: Pickleball Equipment

- Pickleball Paddle: The paddle is typically made of composite materials, wood, or other materials. It must meet size and weight regulations.
- Pickleball Ball: Pickleballs are perforated plastic balls available in indoor and outdoor variations.
- Non-Marking Court Shoes: Players should wear non-marking shoes designed for court sports.
- Protective Eyewear (optional): Some players opt to wear protective eyewear, especially when playing outdoors.

Appendix D: Official Rules and Regulations

- The official rulebook for pickleball is published by the USA Pickleball Association (USAPA) and is regularly updated to reflect changes in the sport.

Appendix E: Organizations and Resources

- USA Pickleball Association (USAPA): The national governing body for pickleball in the United States.
- International Federation of Pickleball (IFP): The global governing body for pickleball.
- Local Pickleball Clubs: Many regions have local clubs and organizations dedicated to promoting and growing the sport.

Appendix F: Glossary of Pickleball Terms

- This glossary provides definitions of common pickleball terms and jargon used in the sport.

Appendix G: Additional Reading and References

- A list of books, websites, and other resources for further reading and research on pickleball.

Appendix H: Tournament Schedule and Calendar

- A sample tournament schedule and calendar to help players find and plan their participation in pickleball events.

Appendix I: Blank Score Sheet

- A printable score sheet for use during pickleball matches.

Appendix J: Pickleball Etiquette Guide

- A concise guide to pickleball etiquette for quick reference.

Appendix K: Skill-Building Exercises and Drills

- A selection of skill-building exercises and drills to help players improve their pickleball skills.

Appendix L: Nutrition and Hydration Tips for Pickleball Players

- Information on proper nutrition and hydration for peak pickleball performance.

Appendix M: Injury Prevention and Recovery

- Tips and guidelines for preventing common pickleball injuries and promoting recovery.

Appendix N: Pickleball Variations and Formats

- A list of popular pickleball variations and formats for players looking to explore different aspects of the sport.

Appendix O: Frequently Asked Questions (FAQ)

- A compilation of frequently asked questions about pickleball and their answers for quick reference.

Appendix P: Interviews with Pickleball Legends

- Transcripts of interviews with notable pickleball players and their insights into the sport.

Appendix Q: Conclusion

- A summary of the key takeaways and concluding remarks from the book.

Appendix R: Index

- An index of topics and terms covered in the book for easy reference.

Glossary of Pickleball Terms

1. Ace: A serve that lands in the opponent's court without being touched, resulting in a point.

2. Baseline: The back boundary of the pickleball court.

3. Centerline: The line dividing the left and right service courts.

4. Dink: A soft shot, typically hit from close to the net, intended to clear the net and land softly in the opponent's non-volley zone.

5. Double Bounce Rule: The rule that dictates that each team must allow the ball to bounce once on each side of the net before volleys are permitted.

6. Fault: A violation of the rules, such as a failed serve or stepping into the non-volley zone when volleying.

7. Kitchen: The non-volley zone, a seven-foot area on both sides of the net where volleys are not allowed.

8. Match: A series of games, often played in a best-of-three or best-of-five format, to determine the overall winner.

9. Net Cord: When the ball hits the net but still goes over and into the opponent's court.

10. Non-Volley Zone (NVZ): The area on each side of the net, extending seven feet back from the net, where volleys are not allowed.

11. Pickleball Paddle: The rectangular paddle used to hit the pickleball. Paddles come in various materials and designs.

12. Pickleball Court: The playing area, 20 feet wide and 44 feet long for doubles play, with specific markings for different zones.

13. Poach: In doubles play, when one player crosses over to the partner's side of the court to intercept the ball.

14. Rally: The exchange of shots between two teams until the point is won or lost.

15. Serve: The shot that initiates each point, starting from behind the baseline and diagonally into the opponent's service court.

16. Side-Out: A loss of serve due to a fault, resulting in the opposing team taking over the serve.

17. Singles Play: A pickleball match played with one player on each side, rather than two.

18. Third Shot Drop: A soft shot, often a dink, played as the third shot after the serve and return to set up positioning at the net.

19. Volley: Hitting the ball in the air, before it bounces, often executed at the net.

20. Zero-Zero-2: A common serving sequence in pickleball, where the server announces the score as "Zero-Zero-2" to indicate the serving team's score first, then the receiving team's score, and finally the server's position as the second server.

Pickleball score sheet

TEAM 1

serve	S	S	S
time outs	1	2	3

score	1	1	1
	2	2	2
	3	3	3
	4	4	4
	5	5	5
	6	6	6
	7	7	7
	8	8	8
	9	9	9
	10	10	10
	11	11	11
	12	12	12
	13	13	13
	14	14	14
	15	15	15
	16	16	16
	17	17	17
	18	18	18
	19	19	19
	20	20	20
	21	21	21

TEAM 2

serve	S	S	S
time outs	1	2	3

score	1	1	1
	2	2	2
	3	3	3
	4	4	4
	5	5	5
	6	6	6
	7	7	7
	8	8	8
	9	9	9
	10	10	10
	11	11	11
	12	12	12
	13	13	13
	14	14	14
	15	15	15
	16	16	16
	17	17	17
	18	18	18
	19	19	19
	20	20	20
	21	21	21

WINNERS	Game 1	Game 2	Game 3

Pickleball score sheet

TEAM 1

serve	S	S	S

time outs	1	2	3

score			
	1	1	1
	2	2	2
	3	3	3
	4	4	4
	5	5	5
	6	6	6
	7	7	7
	8	8	8
	9	9	9
	10	10	10
	11	11	11
	12	12	12
	13	13	13
	14	14	14
	15	15	15
	16	16	16
	17	17	17
	18	18	18
	19	19	19
	20	20	20
	21	21	21

TEAM 2

serve	S	S	S

time outs	1	2	3

score			
	1	1	1
	2	2	2
	3	3	3
	4	4	4
	5	5	5
	6	6	6
	7	7	7
	8	8	8
	9	9	9
	10	10	10
	11	11	11
	12	12	12
	13	13	13
	14	14	14
	15	15	15
	16	16	16
	17	17	17
	18	18	18
	19	19	19
	20	20	20
	21	21	21

WINNERS	Game 1	Game 2	Game 3

Pickleball score sheet

TEAM 1					TEAM 2			
serve	S	S	S		serve	S	S	S

time outs	1	2	3		time outs	1	2	3

score	1	1	1		score	1	1	1
	2	2	2			2	2	2
	3	3	3			3	3	3
	4	4	4			4	4	4
	5	5	5			5	5	5
	6	6	6			6	6	6
	7	7	7			7	7	7
	8	8	8			8	8	8
	9	9	9			9	9	9
	10	10	10			10	10	10
	11	11	11			11	11	11
	12	12	12			12	12	12
	13	13	13			13	13	13
	14	14	14			14	14	14
	15	15	15			15	15	15
	16	16	16			16	16	16
	17	17	17			17	17	17
	18	18	18			18	18	18
	19	19	19			19	19	19
	20	20	20			20	20	20
	21	21	21			21	21	21

WINNERS	Game 1	Game 2	Game 3

Pickleball score sheet

TEAM 1			
serve	S	S	S

time outs	1	2	3

score	1	1	1
	2	2	2
	3	3	3
	4	4	4
	5	5	5
	6	6	6
	7	7	7
	8	8	8
	9	9	9
	10	10	10
	11	11	11
	12	12	12
	13	13	13
	14	14	14
	15	15	15
	16	16	16
	17	17	17
	18	18	18
	19	19	19
	20	20	20
	21	21	21

TEAM 2			
serve	S	S	S

time outs	1	2	3

score	1	1	1
	2	2	2
	3	3	3
	4	4	4
	5	5	5
	6	6	6
	7	7	7
	8	8	8
	9	9	9
	10	10	10
	11	11	11
	12	12	12
	13	13	13
	14	14	14
	15	15	15
	16	16	16
	17	17	17
	18	18	18
	19	19	19
	20	20	20
	21	21	21

WINNERS	Game 1	Game 2	Game 3

Pickleball score sheet

TEAM 1			
serve	S	S	S

time outs	1	2	3

score	1	1	1
	2	2	2
	3	3	3
	4	4	4
	5	5	5
	6	6	6
	7	7	7
	8	8	8
	9	9	9
	10	10	10
	11	11	11
	12	12	12
	13	13	13
	14	14	14
	15	15	15
	16	16	16
	17	17	17
	18	18	18
	19	19	19
	20	20	20
	21	21	21

TEAM 2			
serve	S	S	S

time outs	1	2	3

score	1	1	1
	2	2	2
	3	3	3
	4	4	4
	5	5	5
	6	6	6
	7	7	7
	8	8	8
	9	9	9
	10	10	10
	11	11	11
	12	12	12
	13	13	13
	14	14	14
	15	15	15
	16	16	16
	17	17	17
	18	18	18
	19	19	19
	20	20	20
	21	21	21

WINNERS	Game 1	Game 2	Game 3

Pickleball score sheet

TEAM 1			
serve	S	S	S

time outs	1	2	3

score	1	1	1
	2	2	2
	3	3	3
	4	4	4
	5	5	5
	6	6	6
	7	7	7
	8	8	8
	9	9	9
	10	10	10
	11	11	11
	12	12	12
	13	13	13
	14	14	14
	15	15	15
	16	16	16
	17	17	17
	18	18	18
	19	19	19
	20	20	20
	21	21	21

TEAM 2			
serve	S	S	S

time outs	1	2	3

score	1	1	1
	2	2	2
	3	3	3
	4	4	4
	5	5	5
	6	6	6
	7	7	7
	8	8	8
	9	9	9
	10	10	10
	11	11	11
	12	12	12
	13	13	13
	14	14	14
	15	15	15
	16	16	16
	17	17	17
	18	18	18
	19	19	19
	20	20	20
	21	21	21

WINNERS	Game 1	Game 2	Game 3

Pickleball score sheet

TEAM 1			
serve	S	S	S

time outs	1	2	3

score	1	1	1
	2	2	2
	3	3	3
	4	4	4
	5	5	5
	6	6	6
	7	7	7
	8	8	8
	9	9	9
	10	10	10
	11	11	11
	12	12	12
	13	13	13
	14	14	14
	15	15	15
	16	16	16
	17	17	17
	18	18	18
	19	19	19
	20	20	20
	21	21	21

TEAM 2			
serve	S	S	S

time outs	1	2	3

score	1	1	1
	2	2	2
	3	3	3
	4	4	4
	5	5	5
	6	6	6
	7	7	7
	8	8	8
	9	9	9
	10	10	10
	11	11	11
	12	12	12
	13	13	13
	14	14	14
	15	15	15
	16	16	16
	17	17	17
	18	18	18
	19	19	19
	20	20	20
	21	21	21

WINNERS	Game 1	Game 2	Game 3

Pickleball score sheet

TEAM 1					TEAM 2			
serve	S	S	S		serve	S	S	S

time outs	1	2	3		time outs	1	2	3

score					score			
	1	1	1			1	1	1
	2	2	2			2	2	2
	3	3	3			3	3	3
	4	4	4			4	4	4
	5	5	5			5	5	5
	6	6	6			6	6	6
	7	7	7			7	7	7
	8	8	8			8	8	8
	9	9	9			9	9	9
	10	10	10			10	10	10
	11	11	11			11	11	11
	12	12	12			12	12	12
	13	13	13			13	13	13
	14	14	14			14	14	14
	15	15	15			15	15	15
	16	16	16			16	16	16
	17	17	17			17	17	17
	18	18	18			18	18	18
	19	19	19			19	19	19
	20	20	20			20	20	20
	21	21	21			21	21	21

WINNERS	Game 1	Game 2	Game 3

Pickleball score sheet

TEAM 1			
serve	S	S	S

time outs	1	2	3

score	1	1	1
	2	2	2
	3	3	3
	4	4	4
	5	5	5
	6	6	6
	7	7	7
	8	8	8
	9	9	9
	10	10	10
	11	11	11
	12	12	12
	13	13	13
	14	14	14
	15	15	15
	16	16	16
	17	17	17
	18	18	18
	19	19	19
	20	20	20
	21	21	21

TEAM 2			
serve	S	S	S

time outs	1	2	3

score	1	1	1
	2	2	2
	3	3	3
	4	4	4
	5	5	5
	6	6	6
	7	7	7
	8	8	8
	9	9	9
	10	10	10
	11	11	11
	12	12	12
	13	13	13
	14	14	14
	15	15	15
	16	16	16
	17	17	17
	18	18	18
	19	19	19
	20	20	20
	21	21	21

WINNERS	Game 1	Game 2	Game 3

Pickleball score sheet

TEAM 1					TEAM 2			
serve	S	S	S		serve	S	S	S

time outs	1	2	3		time outs	1	2	3

score					score			
	1	1	1			1	1	1
	2	2	2			2	2	2
	3	3	3			3	3	3
	4	4	4			4	4	4
	5	5	5			5	5	5
	6	6	6			6	6	6
	7	7	7			7	7	7
	8	8	8			8	8	8
	9	9	9			9	9	9
	10	10	10			10	10	10
	11	11	11			11	11	11
	12	12	12			12	12	12
	13	13	13			13	13	13
	14	14	14			14	14	14
	15	15	15			15	15	15
	16	16	16			16	16	16
	17	17	17			17	17	17
	18	18	18			18	18	18
	19	19	19			19	19	19
	20	20	20			20	20	20
	21	21	21			21	21	21

WINNERS	Game 1	Game 2	Game 3

Pickleball score sheet

TEAM 1			
serve	S	S	S

time outs	1	2	3

score	1	1	1
	2	2	2
	3	3	3
	4	4	4
	5	5	5
	6	6	6
	7	7	7
	8	8	8
	9	9	9
	10	10	10
	11	11	11
	12	12	12
	13	13	13
	14	14	14
	15	15	15
	16	16	16
	17	17	17
	18	18	18
	19	19	19
	20	20	20
	21	21	21

TEAM 2			
serve	S	S	S

time outs	1	2	3

score	1	1	1
	2	2	2
	3	3	3
	4	4	4
	5	5	5
	6	6	6
	7	7	7
	8	8	8
	9	9	9
	10	10	10
	11	11	11
	12	12	12
	13	13	13
	14	14	14
	15	15	15
	16	16	16
	17	17	17
	18	18	18
	19	19	19
	20	20	20
	21	21	21

WINNERS	Game 1	Game 2	Game 3

Pickleball score sheet

TEAM 1			
serve	S	S	S

time outs	1	2	3

score	1	1	1
	2	2	2
	3	3	3
	4	4	4
	5	5	5
	6	6	6
	7	7	7
	8	8	8
	9	9	9
	10	10	10
	11	11	11
	12	12	12
	13	13	13
	14	14	14
	15	15	15
	16	16	16
	17	17	17
	18	18	18
	19	19	19
	20	20	20
	21	21	21

TEAM 2			
serve	S	S	S

time outs	1	2	3

score	1	1	1
	2	2	2
	3	3	3
	4	4	4
	5	5	5
	6	6	6
	7	7	7
	8	8	8
	9	9	9
	10	10	10
	11	11	11
	12	12	12
	13	13	13
	14	14	14
	15	15	15
	16	16	16
	17	17	17
	18	18	18
	19	19	19
	20	20	20
	21	21	21

WINNERS	Game 1	Game 2	Game 3